The Role of Critical Success Factors in Six Sigma Implementation: The Case of a City Government

Chamith Wasage, DBA

Acknowledgements

I would like to express my sincere gratitude to my friends, colleagues, and students who provided me prompt guidance and feedback for this book. Your intellectual directions and suggestions helped improve the quality of this book. The knowledge I received from you was truly extraordinary. Also, the dedication of this book goes to my late parents and grandparents. Their unconditional love, intellectual contribution, and support are my motivation to finish this long journey. I want to demonstrate to them that all dreams can be achieved through hard work, persistence, commitment, devotion, and sacrifice.

ABSTRACT

To date, no studies have investigated the influence of critical success factors (CSFs) on Six Sigma implementation in local governments. Research shows that CSFs are those vital elements which are critical to the success of Six Sigma implementation. Without them, Six Sigma projects have little chance of producing net positive results. Thus, the purpose of this research is to conduct a qualitative case study on identified CSF status (relative importance/rank order) during Six Sigma implementation projects in the City of Fort Wayne, IN. Based on the Six Sigma management literature, 11 CSFs were identified and presented to the quality executive officer (respondent/interviewee) in Fort Wayne. The identified CSFs were as follows:

- Leadership commitment to Six Sigma
- Upper management commitment to quality
- Leadership and upper management support of a Six Sigma budget
- Using customers' concerns and feedback to improve quality

- Employee training on project management, statistical tools, quality commitment, teamwork, and DMAIC/DFSS (define, measure, analyze, improve, control/design for Six Sigma)
- Open communication between management and employees of Six Sigma projects
- Providing employee training to Six Sigma belts (Yellow Belt, Green Belt, Black Belt, Master Black Belt, and Champion)
- Offering rewards and recognition for Six Sigma project employees
- Six Sigma training during the hiring process
- Linking Six Sigma to suppliers (software vendors and material providers)
- Training on Six Sigma to reduce employee turnover

The respondent was asked to prioritize (rank order/relative importance using a Likert-scale of 1 = least important, 2 = less important, 3 = important, 4 = very important, 5 = most important) these CSFs based on the respondent's experience in Six Sigma implementation. Results obtained from the case study revealed that "leadership commitment to Six Sigma, upper management commitment to quality, and leadership and upper management support of a Six Sigma budget" were identified as the most important CSFs. Results of the case study also found that "Six Sigma training during the hiring process and training on Six Sigma to reduce employee turnover" were the least important CSFs. These findings were aligned with previous Six Sigma research in private organizations. Thus, analysis showed that rank orders (relative importance) of CSFs on Six Sigma projects in the private and public sectors display similar characteristics. In addition, the analysis revealed that Fort Wayne used Objective Based Budgeting (OBB) and common Six Sigma metrics such as project savings, customer complaints/satisfaction, and production/service delivery time to evaluate the effect of CSFs on the success of Six Sigma-based projects.

Table of Contents

Acknowledgements ii
ABSTRACT iii
List of Figures viii
List of Tables ix
INTRODUCTION 1
Background 1
Statement of the Problem 5
Purpose of the Study 7
Research Questions 9
LITERATURE REVIEW 12
What is a Business Process? 12
What is Six Sigma? 14
Six Sigma in Local Governments 17
Identification of CSFs and Metrics 21
Implementation Roadmap 29
Implementation Structure 32
METHODOLOY 37
Sampling Method 39
Survey Instrument 40
Type of Questions and Design 41
FINDINGS AND DISCUSSION 46

CONCLUSION	61
LIMITATIONS OF THE STUDY	68
References	71
Author Biography	88

List of Figures

Figure

Figure 1: The Process Model 13

Figure 2: Six Sigma Structure 36

List of Tables

Table

Table 1 DMAIC steps 31

Table 2 Rank order of CSFs 49

INTRODUCTION

Background

Local governments, state governments, and federal agencies are at a crossroad today. On one hand, citizens are demanding efficient and effective services from their governments more than ever before (Benest, n.d; Bowman & Kearney, 2010; Edwards, 2011). On the other hand, federal, state, and local governments are confronted by budgetary shortfalls. These revenue and spending imbalances spur downsizing at all levels of government services, especially at the local level (Benest, n.d; Bowman & Kearney, 2010; Edwards, 2011). The budget imbalances of local governments began in the third quarter of 2001 due to extraordinary security measures in the wake of September 11, rising costs of employee health benefits, public safety needs, and capital spending (Sawicky, 2002). In the second quarter of 2002, federal and state governments began to reduce aid to local governments (Sawicky, 2002).

In addition, during the most recent economic recession (from December 2007 to June 2009), local governments faced unprecedented budget downturns due to a reduced level of federal and state aid and decreased local personal, corporate, sales, and property taxes. Despite the economic recession, which officially ended in June 2009, most municipal governments failed to return to their pre-recession revenue and employment levels (House, 2013). The federal sequestration process, an across-the-board spending cut for the fiscal year ending September 30, 2013, has negatively impacted local government budgets. According to the Federal Funds Information for States, under the federal sequestration, local governments received $28.3 billion in fiscal year (FY) 2013, compared to $29.8 billion in fiscal year (FY) 2012 (Lambert, 2013). Moreover, local governments are collectively confronted with a $225 billion structural budget deficit, which constitutes about 12 percent of their total spending (Edwards, 2011). Additionally, since 2006, local governments have eliminated 353,000 jobs, furloughed employees, and refinanced pension obligations (Edwards, 2011).

These financial crises raise many questions: Can local governments do more with less? Can they cut some services? Instead of providing less, can local governments operate more efficiently and effectively to provide more with less? These issues lead to a critical question: How do local governments deliver obligated mission-driven services with limited revenues? "For this reason, there is no better time than now to take a hard look at the efficiency of local governments" (Edwards, 2011, p. 3). Some U.S. local governments, including Fort Wayne, confronted these issues through improving efficiency in their processes (House, 2013).

Although many management theories and strategies are designed to improve efficiency in processes, reduce defects/errors, and increase efficiency, many leading U.S. companies have adopted Six Sigma. Research shows that improving business processes through Six Sigma in fact reduces costs and defects/errors and improves services and quality simultaneously (Anbari & Kwak, 2004; Antony & Banuelas, 2002; Wasage, 2012). Through successful implementation of Six Sigma, research has found that leading U.S. companies such as Motorola, Allied Signal, General Electric, Raytheon, Bank of America, Bechtel, and Caterpillar have reduced their defects and process variation, and increased quality and profitability (Anbari & Kwak, 2004; Antony & Banuelas, 2002; Gillet, Fink, & Bevington, 2010; Greene, Ellis, Waller, & Osborne, 2008). To replicate these success stories in the private sector, some local governments, including Fort Wayne, have implemented Six Sigma in their process operations to increase efficiency and reduce defects. Fort Wayne is one of the early adopters of Six Sigma operations (Robinson, 2001), using Six Sigma in its processes to improve customer service and to increase the effectiveness of its services (Furterer & Elshennawy, 2005; Richard, 2005).

Statement of the Problem

To date, the empirical evidence is mixed regarding the impact of Six Sigma in both the private (Wasage, 2012) and public sectors (Pyzdek, 2014). "The success and failure of most Six Sigma programmes largely depend upon their implementation rather than their contents" (Moosa & Sajid, 2010, p. 747). According to the business management literature (Antony, 2004), to successfully implement Six Sigma projects, organizations must utilize Critical Success Factors (CSFs). Research shows that CSFs are the essential ingredients for the success of Six Sigma projects because if these factors do not exist during the implementation, Six Sigma projects may not produce expected positive results (Antony, 2004; J. Antony, F.J. Antony, Kumar, & Cho, 2007; Kundi, 2005). If CSFs are not present during the Six Sigma project implementation, organizations will waste resources such as money and time (Antony, Kumar, & Labib, 2008). The evidence suggests that many authors (Antony, 2004; J. Antony et al., 2007; Antony et al.,

2008; Antony & Banuelas, 2002; Coronado & Antony, 2002; Kundi, 2005; Tran, 2006; Wasage, 2012) have examined CSFs for successfully implementing Six Sigma in private organizations, but no study has investigated the influence of CSFs on Six Sigma implementation in local governments. Thus, this topic needs further academic investigation to fill the gap.

Six Sigma scholars argue that "if the corporation fails to obtain these Critical Success Factors, then the corporation will experience significant failures" (Ho & Chuang 2006, p. 171). It is also essential to understand and identify the most important and least important (prioritized order/relative importance order/rank order) CSFs because such identification will help managers develop an appropriate resource allocation plan (Antony et al., 2008). Also, managers should ensure that the implementation produces anticipated bottom line financial and non-financial benefits. Thus, it is also recommended that managers use Six Sigma metrics to evaluate anticipated implementation success.

Purpose of the Study

Research shows that through successful Six Sigma implementation, government agencies can increase the quality of the services provided and reduce process variation (Ho & Chuang, 2006). A review of previous literature, however, found that scholars have shown little interest in conducting a study on the influence of CSFs on Six Sigma implementation in local governments (Furterer & Elshennawy, 2005) because the vast majority of Six Sigma implementation research has been conducted in large manufacturing companies (Antony, 2004; J. Antony et al., 2007; Furterer & Elshennawy, 2005).

Literature shows that there are some CSF and Six Sigma implementation studies in the private sector (Antony, 2004; Antony et al., 2007; Antony et al., 2008; Antony & Banuelas, 2002; Coronado & Antony, 2002; Kundi, 2005; Wasage, 2012). No studies, however, investigated the influence of CSFs on Six Sigma implementation in local governments. Thus, this topic needs to be thoroughly explored. Since identification of CSFs is the key ingredient for the successful implementation of Six Sigma initiatives (Antony, 2004; Antony & Banuelas, 2002; J. Antony et al., 2007; Antony et al., 2008), the purpose of this research is to conduct a qualitative case study on identified CSF status (prioritized/relative importance/rank order) during the Six Sigma implementation projects in the City of Fort Wayne, IN.

This study is not only contributing to the Six Sigma literature in Public Administration, it also pragmatically helps Six Sigma project managers prioritize and allocate resources based on CSFs. This could lead to achievements in operational excellence through successful Six Sigma implementation (Antony, 2004; Antony & Banuelas, 2002; J. Antony et al, 2007; Antony et al., 2008). As indicated above, most Six Sigma research was conducted and viewed from manufacturing industry perspectives. This study, however, investigates Six Sigma implementation in a government service organization; thus, this research provides a framework for a paradigm shift.

Research Questions

Based on the statement of the problem and purpose of the study, the following research questions (RQ) will be critically investigated:

RQ 1. To what extent does Fort Wayne use CSFs in the implementation of Six Sigma projects?

RQ 2. How does Fort Wayne prioritize CSFs if the city deems them important components of Six Sigma implementation?

RQ 3. What are the effects of CSFs in the success of Six Sigma-based projects?

Based on the research questions, the following hypotheses (H) are proposed:

H1. Leadership commitment Six Sigma is the most important CSF in public sector Six Sigma-based projects.

H2. Relative importance (rank) orders of CSFs on Six Sigma projects in the private and public sectors display similar characteristics.

The literature suggests that Fort Wayne used Six Sigma (initiated in 2000 and finished in 2008) in its processes and the city launched 60 Six Sigma projects in the first three years of Six Sigma deployment (Maleyeff, 2007; Richard, 2005). Thus, the research questions will be analyzed using public data and phone interviews with city officials who worked in Six Sigma projects in Fort Wayne. However, for this study, CSF effects focus on holistic operational matters (all projects' impact), rather than a particular project (one project) planning (Antony et al., 2008). In other words, the research focuses on the influence of CSFs in Six Sigma implementation (holistic approach) in Fort Wayne.

The remainder of this case study is organized as follows. First, to build a foundation for the research questions and for the purpose of this study, a review of previous relevant literature is presented (Antony et al., 2008; Tran, 2006). This is followed by a methodology section to describe the research approach, design, and data collection. The findings section is next. The final section presents the conclusions and summary, discusses limitations of the study, and presents recommendations for further research (Antony et al., 2008; Tran, 2006).

LITERATURE REVIEW
What is a Business Process?

Six Sigma helps reduce process variation. Every organization has a business process to create value (Jones, 1999; Turban, Sharda, Aronson, & King, 2008) which consists of inputs, conversion (process), and outputs. Therefore, a process is a series of activities that transform inputs into outputs (Jones, 1999; Turban et al., 2008). The graphical representation of the process model is depicted below:

Inputs: raw materials, money and capital, human resources, information, and knowledge.

Conversion/process: machinery, computers, and human skills.

Outputs: finished goods and services, salaries, dividends, and value to stakeholders (Jones, 1999).

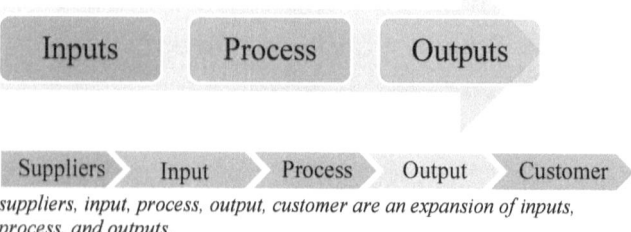

suppliers, input, process, output, customer are an expansion of inputs, process, and outputs.

Figure 1: The Process Model

Most inefficiency and defects occur in the process (Wasage, 2012). Inefficiency appears if an organization fails to use the lowest amount of inputs to generate the highest amount of outputs (Antony, 2004; Antony & Banuelas, 2002; J. Antony et al, 2007; Antony et al., 2008). A defect can be defined from many perspectives, but is basically a product or service that does not meet customer/client expectations (Antony, 2004; Antony & Banuelas, 2002; J. Antony et al, 2007; Antony et al., 2008). A defect can vary from a major damaged part in airline manufacturing operations to an inaccurate customer billing statement in local government operations (Antony, 2004; Antony & Banuelas, 2002; J. Antony et al, 2007; Antony et al., 2008; Wasage, 2012). Business research shows that the lack of product quality, or not doing things correctly the first time, could cost companies 15 to 40 percent of total annual sales revenue (Buthmann, 2010).

What is Six Sigma?

Six Sigma was first introduced at Motorola in the mid-1980s to improve performance of its processes (Antony et al., 2008). The foundation of Six Sigma is based on Edward Deming's database process improvement methodology of Plan, Do, Check, Act, or P-D-C-A (Deming, 1986; Pande, Neuman, & Cavanagh, 2000). Six Sigma is a statistical methodology that identifies process variation. Six Sigma is also a management strategy that helps improve product/service quality, customer satisfaction, profitability, and productivity (Antony, 2004; Antony & Banuelas, 2002; J. Antony et al, 2007; Antony et al., 2008; Wasage, 2012). Pavletic and Sokovic (2002) defined Six Sigma as a quality improvement program, whereas other scholars describe Six Sigma as a business process improvement methodology (Turban et al., 2008).

Six Sigma can be defined from two perspectives: statistical expressions and management terms. From a statistical perspective, "Six Sigma uses the Greek letter "sigma" (σ) to represent a standard deviation away from the mean. The sixth sigma is a representation of six standard deviations away from the mean of the population" (Gillett et al., 2010, p. 26). In a normal statistical distribution, the standard deviation represents a measure of variability or inconsistency, which demonstrates how all data points vary from the mean value (average) or the process average (Antony & Banuelas, 2002; Gupta, 2013; Wasage, 2012).

In Six Sigma, customer specifications such as lower specification limit (LSL) and upper specification limit (USL) are six standard deviations from the process mean value. Since the process is subject to variation, the process mean could shift as much as 1.5 standard deviation off the target (Hekmatpanah, Sadroddin, Shahbaz, Mokhtari, & Fadavinia, 2008), "factoring a shift of 1.5 standard deviation in the process mean then results in a 3.4

DPMO" (Hekmatpanah et al., 2008, p. 732). Statistically, the objective of Six Sigma is to keep the distance between the process average and the nearest tolerance limit to at least six standard deviations, thus helping to reduce variability in products and processes (Antony et al., 2008).

From the management perspective, Six Sigma is a project-driven management strategy that reduces defects, eliminates waste, enhances financial performance, improves product and service quality, and improves customer/client satisfaction (Antony et al., 2008; Antony & Banuelas, 2002; Anbari & Kwak, 2004; Furterer & Elshennawy, 2005; Harry & Schroeder, 2000; Shah, Chandrasekaran, & Linderman, 2008). Although many definitions and perspectives are associated with Six Sigma, the primary objectives of Six Sigma remain the same, driving out waste/defects/errors to increase profitability, improve savings, enhance customer/client satisfaction, and improve the quality of products and services (Antony & Banuelas, 2002). Improved service and product quality is critical for any organization, and according to the City of Fort Wayne website, the city implemented Six Sigma to improve its customer service and increase the effectiveness of the city services (Furterer & Elshennawy, 2005).

Six Sigma in Local Governments

Fort Wayne is one of the early adopters of Six Sigma operations (Robinson, 2001), using Six Sigma in its processes to improve customer service and to increase the effectiveness of its services (Furterer & Elshennawy, 2005; Richard, 2005). Fort Wayne former Mayor Graham Richard (2000-2008) began implementing Six Sigma in the city in 2000. Prior to Six Sigma implementation in the city government, there was little use of information (analysis of data) in government agencies, little awareness of process flow, and information of customer needs/satisfaction (George, 2003).

To deploy Six Sigma, Mayor Richard established an executive council to monitor Six Sigma implementation in the city (George, 2003).

The executive council's responsibility was to design a plan to get the new methods deployed into city government: how many Black Belts the city wanted to have trained, the kind of projects these Black Belts should work on, and what department they would come from (George, 2003). The city launched 60 Six Sigma projects in the first three years of Six Sigma deployment, including projects in the Fire, Public Service, Transportation, and Park Departments. Mayor Richard also created a new position (Quality Enhancement Manager) to supervise the Six Sigma projects in city operations (City of Fort Wayne, 2007; George, 2003).

While the majority of the research investigating Six Sigma implementation has occurred in the manufacturing sector, few recent studies have been conducted on public organizations. These studies failed to examine the influence of CSFs on Six Sigma implementation in local governments. Maleyeff (2007) examined the effect of Six Sigma implementation on the City of Hartford's tax collection process and Oregon's Lane

County safety procedures. In both instances, improvements were found following implementation of Lean Six Sigma (Maleyeff, 2007). Lean Six Sigma's main objective is to drive out waste, whereas Six Sigma focuses on reducing process variation (Antony, 2004; Antony & Banuelas, 2002; J. Antony et al, 2007; Antony et al., 2008; Maleyeff, 2007).

The City of Coral Springs, Florida implemented Total Quality Management (TQM) programs to completely overhaul operations and service delivery (City of Coral Springs, 2014). The city won the Florida Governor's Sterling Award in 1997 and again in 2003. The award is based on the Malcolm Baldrige organizational excellence of customer and market focus, leadership, strategic planning, information analysis, human resources focus, and process management and business results (City of Coral Springs, 2014; Furterer & Elshennaway, 2005).

The City of Kingsport, Tennessee received a grant from the American Society for Quality (ASQ) for its Six Sigma projects (Furterer & Elshennaway, 2005). Kingsport public workers used Six Sigma to improve trash collection services. Research shows that Six Sigma implementation resulted in more than 50 process improvements to daily operations, $86,000 in direct budget reductions, $42,500 in cost savings, and $50,000 in productivity recoveries (Center for Association Leadership, 2011).

Furterer and Elshennaway (2005) and Boyne and Walker (2002) investigated how TQM was utilized in private and public organizations and whether TQM helped improve performance in these organizations. Hellein and Bowman (2002) also studied the impact of the implementation of quality management in Florida state government agencies. Additionally, Furterer and Elshennaway (2005) studied TQM and Lean Six Sigma implementation tools in a local government, focusing on implementing TQM and Lean Six Sigma tools to improve services in a local government. Researchers (Furterer & Elshennaway, 2005) used the DMAIC (define, measure, analyze, improve, control) problem solving methodology to improve financial processes.

The above research (Boyne & Walker, 2002; Furterer & Elshennaway, 2005; Hellein & Bowman, 2002) mainly investigated TQM in public organizations, yet failed to investigate CSFs for implementing Six Sigma in local governments or to evaluate the implementation success using Six Sigma metrics. Thus, this research will address some shortcomings in the existing Six Sigma literature. In order to determine CSFs and Six Sigma metrics, the next section will explore some related Six Sigma studies.

Identification of CSFs and Metrics

CSFs are those vital components which are critical to the success of Six Sigma implementation (Coronado & Antony, 2002). Without these CSFs, projects have little chance of obtaining positive net results (Coronado & Antony, 2002). Thus, using existing literature, this study compiles the 11 most cited CSFs and five Six Sigma metrics for the effective implementation of Six Sigma projects. The following 11 common CSFs have been identified:

- Leadership commitment to Six Sigma
- Upper management commitment to quality
- Leadership and upper management support of Six Sigma budget
- Using customers' concerns and feedback to improve quality
- Employee training on project management, statistical tools, quality commitment, teamwork, and DMAIC/DFSS (define, measure, analyze, improve, control/design for Six Sigma)
- Open communication between management and employees of Six Sigma projects
- Providing employee training to Six Sigma belts (Yellow Belt, Green Belt, Black Belt, Master Black Belt, and Champion)
- Offering rewards and recognition for Six Sigma project employees
- Six Sigma training during the hiring process

- Linking Six Sigma to suppliers (software vendors and material providers)
- Training on Six Sigma to reduce employee turnover (Anbari & Kwak, 2004; Antony, 2004; Antony et al., 2007; Antony et al., 2008; Antony & Banuelas, 2002; Coronado & Antony, 2002; Eckes, 2000; Kundi, 2005; Moosa & Sajid, 2010; Pande et al., 2000; Wasage, 2012).

Research conducted on CSFs and Six Sigma implementation in UK service organizations showed that leadership commitment to Six Sigma, upper management commitment to quality, and employee training on project management skills were the "most important" CSFs (Antony, 2004). The analysis also indicated that offering rewards and recognition to Six Sigma project employees were "important" factors (Antony, 2004). A similar study by Antony et al. (2007) found that customer focus, leadership commitment to Six Sigma, upper management commitment to quality, and employee training on project management skills were "very important"

CSFs. In addition, project tracking reviews and Six Sigma training and education were rated as "important" CSFs (Antony et al., 2007). On the other hand, incentive programs for Six Sigma projects were "less important" (Antony et al., 2007).

These findings were supported by a survey of Canadian Six Sigma manufacturing firms in which Tran (2006) asked respondents to identify the three most important CSFs for successful Six Sigma implementation. From the response analysis, Tran (2006) found that the following CSFs were the three "most important" factors in the successful implementation of Six Sigma: managerial involvement and commitment, integrating Six Sigma into business, and Six Sigma training. Chakraborty and Tan (2012) also found that top management commitment to Six Sigma, education and training, and cultural change were the "most important" CSFs.

In a survey of CSFs for the successful implementation of Six Sigma projects within small UK manufacturing enterprises, Antony et al. (2008) discovered that management involvement and participation and linking Six Sigma customers were the "most important" factors for the successful implementation of Six Sigma. These findings were aligned with Kundi's (2005) research of Six Sigma implementation and CSFs. Kundi (2005) also found that top management support, creating an effective culture change, and effective communication were the "most important" CSFs. These findings were supported by a recent study (Naslund, 2013) of CSFs and Six Sigma implementation. In addition, Naslund (2013) and Achanga (2006) noted four major factors for the successful implementation of Lean and Six Sigma in small to medium businesses: leadership and management, finance (budget), organizational culture, and skills and expertise. Anbari and Kwak (2004) also emphasized management commitment to Six Sigma initiatives, organizational involvement, continuous training, and cultural change as the major CSFs for the success of Six Sigma projects.

In another study of CSFs and Six Sigma implementation, Antony and Banuelas (2002) found that leadership commitment to Six Sigma and upper management commitment to quality were the "most important" CSFs. Antony and Banuelas (2002) also noted that linking Six Sigma to employee training and linking Six Sigma to suppliers were "important" CSFs. Jones, Parast, and Adams (2011) supported these findings and claimed that human resource management practices, top management commitment, and Six Sigma training significantly affected Six Sigma implementation. These findings were aligned with another Six Sigma research study conducted by Wasage (2012). In the survey, Wasage (2012) found that leadership commitment to Six Sigma, upper management commitment to quality, leadership and upper management allocating of financial resources for Six Sigma, and customers' concerns and feedback were highly rated for the successful implementation of Six Sigma, followed by employee training on various techniques (such as project management, statistical tools, teamwork, quality commitment training, and DMAIC/DMADV/DFSS), and ongoing open communication between employees and management about Six Sigma achievements. These findings were also aligned with other Six Sigma practitioners' and scholars' propositions (Eckes, 2000; Harry & Schroeder, 2000; Pande et al., 2000).

CSFs are often regarded as a harbinger of Six Sigma implementation success. Six Sigma metrics, however, can be used to evaluate anticipated implementation success in a Six Sigma project. Most cited Six Sigma metrics include defect rate, financial measures (cost of quality, savings on rework and inspection costs, revenues, profits, return on assets), customer satisfaction/customer complaints, and quality of products/services, and production/service delivery time (Antony, 2004; Antony & Banuelas, 2002; Gillett et al., 2010; Ho & Chuang, 2006; Wasage, 2012). A survey conducted by Antony et al. (2007) indicated that most Six Sigma service organizations used the following metrics to evaluate anticipated implementation success: cost of poor quality (COPQ), defects per million opportunities (DPMO), time to respond to customer complaints, process capability, and number of customer complaints.

Another research study by Tran (2006) found that most Canadian Six Sigma companies used the following metrics: financial measures, DPMO, customer satisfaction, and internal work processes (delivery time, time to respond to complaints). Tran (2006) also discovered that there were statistically significant correlations between CSFs and Six Sigma metrics. There was also a statistically significant correlation between management support and commitment to Six Sigma and financial measures. In addition, there was a statistically significant correlation between management support and commitment to Six Sigma and internal work processes. Moreover, there was a strong statistical correlation between financing Six Sigma (budget for Six Sigma) and internal work processes (Tran, 2006). Wasage (2012) also discovered that there was a positive statistical relationship between linking Six Sigma to human resources (employee training) and productivity (internal work processes).

Identification and prioritization of CSFs will help an organization develop an appropriate implementation plan and a proper resource allocation strategy (Tran, 2006). As a result, if CSFs are present, the implementation of Six Sigma is more likely to succeed (Wasage, 2012). The anticipated success, however, can be evaluated using Six Sigma metrics.

Implementation Roadmap

Six Sigma can be implemented in two approaches: DMAIC (define, measure, analyze, improve, and control) and/or DFSS (design for Six Sigma). DMAIC is the most cited and adopted methodology in Six Sigma implementation (Tjahjono et al., 2010; Wasage, 2012) and it is considered to be an improvement method for existing processes falling below Six Sigma level and requiring incremental improvement (Tjahjono et al., 2010). This methodology is a better selection for focusing on cost reduction, retrenchment or divestiture (Tjahjono et al., 2010; Wasage, 2012).

The Six Sigma roadmap can be defined as a step-by-step methodology for Six Sigma implementation. The following table indicates the DMAIC step methodology:

Table 1
DMAIC steps

DMAIC steps	Description
Define	Define the requirements and expectations of the customer.
	Define the project boundaries.
	Define the process by mapping the business flow.
Measure	Measure the process to satisfy customers' needs.
	Develop a data collection plan.
	Collect and compare data to determine issues and shortfalls.
Analyze	Analyze the causes of defects and sources of variation.
	Determine the variations in the process.
	Prioritize opportunities for future improvement.
Improve	Improve the process to eliminate variations.
	Develop creative alternatives and implement enhanced plan.
Control	Control process variations to meet customer requirements.
	Develop a strategy to monitor and control the improved process.
	Implement the improvements of systems and structures.

Source: Adopted from Hekmatpanah, Sadroddin, Shahbaz, Mokhtari, & Fadavinia, 2008, p. 367.

On the other hand, DFSS is designed to develop new processes or new products at the Six Sigma level. Thus, DFSS can be better used in companies that have strong market growth and competitive position because DFSS focuses on new product development and innovation (Tjahjono et al., 2010; Wasage, 2012). Watson and deYong (2010) defined DFSS as "a process to define, design, and deliver innovative products proved competitively attractive value to customers in a manner that achieves the critical-to-quality characteristics for all the significant factions" (as cited in Tjahjono et al., 2010, p. 220-221).

Implementation Structure

Six Sigma projects are governed by a Six Sigma organizational structure and most organizations use a Six Sigma hierarchy structure to coach and train their employees who work in Six Sigma projects (Anbari & Kwak, 2004; Ho & Chuang, 2006; Pande et al., 2000). The structure consists of five belt certifications: Yellow Belt (YB), Green Belt (GB), Black Belt (BB), Master Black Belt

(MBB), and Champion and Project Sponsor (Anbari & Kwak, 2004; Ho & Chuang, 2006; Pande et al., 2000). Each certified belt includes appropriate training, roles, and responsibilities. Thus, lower level certified individuals are expected to report to higher level certified individuals with issues and problems. In addition, higher level certified individuals are responsible for mentoring and managing lower level individuals to accomplish project objectives. As a result, the belt system helps organizations manage and monitor Six Sigma projects from concept to completion (Anbari & Kwak, 2004).

YBs receive training on the fundamentals of Six Sigma and work part-time on Six Sigma projects and activities (Anbari & Kwak, 2004, Wasage, 2012). YBs typically have basic knowledge of Six Sigma and they do not lead Six Sigma projects, rather they play a supporting role. GBs receive approximately two or three weeks of training on Six Sigma quality management, problem solving skills with the DMAIC model, and performance indicators

(Anbari & Kwak, 2004; Ho & Chuang, 2006; Pande et al., 2000). GBs typically complete Six Sigma projects as normal daily tasks and usually assist BB members. BBs are the project leaders. The Six Sigma project structure is centered on the Black Belt (Anbari & Kwak, 2004). BBs receive extensive training on the DMAIC/DFSS models and Six Sigma statistics. In addition, BBs focus on project execution, monitor project progress, and provide guidance for GBs. BBs typically complete five to ten projects per year (Anbari & Kwak, 2004; Ho & Chuang, 2006).

MBBs are experienced BBs who provide technical support to BBs, GBs, and YBs. Typically, MBBs provide monitoring, mentoring, coaching, and consulting to Six Sigma project members. MBBs report directly to the Champion, thus, they play a managerial and communication role between the corporate executive level and the project teams (Ho & Chuang, 2006). MBBs focus on setting goal targets, allocating resources, and monitoring progress of Six Sigma projects (Ho & Chuang,

2006). Champions are the senior executives who have received the complete Six Sigma training. They play a major role in choosing and sponsoring specific Six Sigma projects (Anbari & Kwak, 2004; Ho & Chuang, 2006; Pande et al., 2000). Champions are also responsible for mitigating and removing roadblocks such as resistance to change, and developing a plan for change management (Anbari & Kwak, 2004; Ho & Chuang, 2006). Champions' main responsibilities include creating the vision, approving projects, reviewing progress, and selecting BBs (Anbari & Kwak, 2004; Ho & Chuang, 2006).

The following graph illustrates a graphical representation of the Six Sigma structure pyramid:

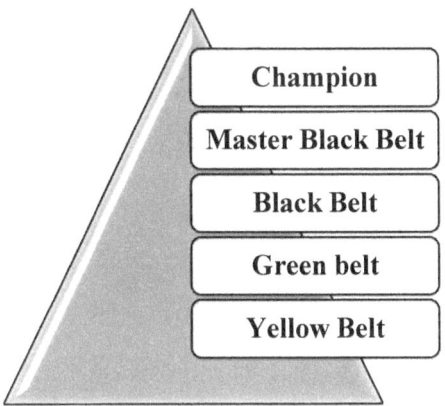

Figure 2: Six Sigma Structure

METHODOLOY

To date, no case studies have investigated the influence of CSFs on Six Sigma implementation in local governments. The purpose of this research is to conduct a qualitative case study on identified CSF status (relative importance/rank order) during the Six Sigma implementation projects in the City of Fort Wayne, IN. Based on the purpose of the study, the following research questions (RQ) will be critically investigated:

RQ 1. To what extent does Fort Wayne use CSFs in the implementation of Six Sigma projects?

RQ 2. How does Fort Wayne prioritize CSFs if the city deems them important components of Six Sigma implementation?

RQ 3. What are the effects of CSFs in the success of Six Sigma based projects?

The qualitative case study method is employed for this research and does not produce statistical data. Qualitative research is useful in defining an issue in order to identify the most significant forces shaping outcomes and results

(Babbie, 1986; Luengo, 2004). Babbie (1986) argued that the central and dominant objective of any research was to systematically explain and predict discipline-specific phenomena. "In the case of most qualitative research, explanation rather than prediction is predominant" (Luengo, 2004, p. 45).

Case studies are useful for analyzing a current real-world context (Yin, 2003). "Case studies contribute to the knowledge of individual, organizational, social, and political occurrences and allow the scholar to retain the holistic and meaningful characteristics of organizational and managerial processes" (Mukkamala, 2013, p. 91). According to Yin (2003), a single case study is appropriate when it is extreme or unique, or it represents a critical case for testing well-formulated theory. A case study can be helpful in research as it aims to explore the deeper meaning of areas already researched and the emerging areas that have not been fully discovered (Hartley, 2004; Mukkamala, 2013). The case study method is also appropriate when research questions embody an explanatory component, such as in this study (i.e., the influence of CSFs on Six Sigma implementation in local governments) (Chakraborty & Tan, 2012; Yin, 2003).

Sampling Method

Six Sigma implementation in the City of Fort Wayne, IN has been selected for the case study. Fort Wayne is one of few local governments that has implemented Six Sigma. Fort Wayne is Indiana's second largest city, with over 258,000 residents in 2014. The city has a Mayor-Council form of government. Fort Wayne introduced Six Sigma in 2000. The city launched 60 Six Sigma projects in the first three years of Six Sigma deployment, including projects in the Fire, Public Service, Transportation, and Park Departments (George, 2003). The Mayor of Fort Wayne created a new position (Quality Enhancement Manager) to supervise the Six Sigma projects in the city operations (George, 2003).

According to the literature, currently, few local governments are using Six Sigma. Fort Wayne, however, is one of the early adopters of Six Sigma operations (Robinson, 2001), using Six Sigma in its processes to improve customer service and to increase the effectiveness of its services (Furterer & Elshennawy, 2005; Richard, 2005). Due to limited control over the choice of the Six Sigma projects in local governments, a convenience sampling technique was used for selecting a local government (Kundi, 2005).

Survey Instrument

In order to achieve research objectives, five quality professionals were contacted via email and telephone. All five target respondents were directly involved in the process of Six Sigma implementation in the city government. After follow-up telephone calls to each target respondent, four target respondents declined to participate in the case study. Thus, a telephone interview was conducted with a quality professional who engaged in the city's 60 Six Sigma implementation projects. The participant (interviewee) had a vast amount of understanding, knowledge, and practical experience with Six Sigma implementation in Fort Wayne. Interviews are particularly useful for gathering information rapidly, getting the story behind a participant's experiences, and asking follow up questions (Valenzuela & Shrivastava, n.d). This particular interview had the following focused characteristics:

1. A participant was known to be involved in the all 60 Six Sigma implementation projects in Fort Wayne.

2. The situation (Six Sigma implementation in Fort Wayne) was analyzed prior to the interview by the principal researcher (interviewer).

3. The interview was focused on the participant's experiences regarding the situation under study (Nachmias & Nachmias, 1996).

Type of Questions and Design

For this research, the open-ended and close-ended question formats were selected. A review of the literature shows that most previous Six Sigma CSF research used these formats (Antony et al., 2008; Kundi, 2005; Wasage, 2012). In the open-ended format, the participant was given an opportunity to discuss the Six Sigma project operation experiences in Fort Wayne. The discussion was focused on a holistic operational approach of Six Sigma implementation rather than a particular project-based approach. Within this format, the participant discussed how Fort Wayne used CSFs and metrics in the implementation of Six Sigma and the effect of CSFs on the success of Six Sigma-based projects.

In the closed-ended format, the participant was offered a set of response categories. From these response categories, the participant was asked to select the one that most closely represents the participant's view (Nachmias & Nachmias, 1996). According to Nachmias and Nachmias (1996), when the objective is to obtain information regarding the degree of importance, ranking can be used in questionnaires. Researchers (Antony et al., 2007; Antony et al., 2008; Kundi, 2005; Wasage, 2012) in the past have used a rating scale (Likert scale of 1 to 5) to identify the relative importance of CSFs. Thus, for this research, a rating scale (Likert scale of 1 to 5) was utilized within the closed-ended question format to obtain answers from the participant.

The primary objective of this research was to conduct a case study on identified CSF status (relative importance/rank order) during the implementation of Six Sigma projects in the City of Fort Wayne, IN. Based on this objective, the following hypothesizes were generated:

H1. Leadership commitment Six Sigma is the most important CSF in public sector Six Sigma based projects and

H2. Relative importance (rank order) of CSFs on Six Sigma projects in the private and public sectors displays similar characteristics.

People in the highest level of the organization/upper management should lead Six Sigma implementation because they possess great influence to change the attitude of the employees towards Six Sigma (Coronado & Antony, 2002). Any successful initiative like Six Sigma requires top leadership commitment. Without top leadership involvement, commitment, support, and motivation, the Six Sigma projects will be in an uncertain position and the effort behind the projects will be weakened (Coronado & Antony, 2002; Pande et al., 2000). Leadership in Fort Wayne strongly advocated team building, applied DMAIC, encouraged learning and training, and required data collecting and analyzing (George, 2003).

To achieve the primary research objective (conduct a case study on identified CSF status during the implementation of Six Sigma projects in Fort Wayne), the participant was asked to identify the 11 CSFs (as identified above) in a rank order to determine the factors most important to the successful implementation of Six Sigma. The 11 CSFs were based on extensive literature review (Anbari & Kwak, 2004; Antony, 2004; Antony et al., 2007; Antony et al., 2008; Antony & Banuelas, 2002; Coronado & Antony, 2002; Eckes, 2000; Kundi, 2005; Moosa & Sajid, 2010; Pande et al., 2000; Wasage, 2012). The close-ended questions (the participant was asked to rank the given CSFs based on the relative importance) and the rating scale were also based on the published Six Sigma literature

(Antony & Banuelas, 2002; Antony et al., 2007; Antony et al., 2008; Eckes, 2000; Kundi, 2005; Wasage, 2012). The following rating scale was used for the rank order:

1 = least important, 2 = less important, 3 = important, 4 = very important, 5 = most important.

FINDINGS AND DISCUSSION

During the interview process, the respondent recognized the following common CSFs and discussed the usage of these CSFs.

- Leadership commitment to Six Sigma
- Upper management commitment to quality
- Leadership and upper management support of Six Sigma budget
- Using customers' concerns and feedback to improve quality
- Employee training on project management, statistical tools, quality commitment, teamwork, and DMAIC/DFSS
- Open communication between management and employees of Six Sigma projects
- Providing employee training to Six Sigma belts (Yellow Belt, Green Belt, Black Belt, Master Black Belt, and Champion)
- Offering rewards and recognition for Six Sigma project employees
- Six Sigma training during the hiring process

- Linking Six Sigma to suppliers (software vendors and material providers)
- Training on Six Sigma to reduce employee turnover (Antony, 2004; Antony et al., 2007; Antony et al., 2008; Antony & Banuelas, 2002; Anbari & Kwak, 2004; Coronado & Antony, 2002; Eckes, 2000; Kundi, 2005; Moosa & Sajid, 2010; Pande et al., 2000; Wasage, 2012).

The respondent noted that all factors were significant and the city used these CSFs during its Six Sigma implementation. The respondent was directly involved in Six Sigma implementation in the city and had first-hand knowledge of experience with Six Sigma projects, and also recognized that to allocate resources properly and to successfully implement Six Sigma, leaders/project managers prioritized these CSFs. The respondent was asked to prioritize/rate (relative importance) given CSFs based on the respondent's experiences, knowledge, and understanding of Six Sigma projects in the City of Fort Wayne, IN. As noted above, the following rating scale was used for the rank order: 1 = least important, 2 = less important, 3 = important, 4 = very important, 5 = most important. Table 2 illustrates scores (relative importance/rank order) of each CSF. The higher the score, the greater the importance of the CSF (Antony et al., 2008).

Table 2
Rank order of CSFs

Critical Success Factor (CSF)	This research rating (based on the respondent experience)	This research rating (based on the respondent experience)	Previous research Rating (mostly, in business organizations)	Previous authorship (mostly, in business organization)
Leadership commitment to Six Sigma	5	Most Important	Similar	(Achanga, 2006; Antony, 2004; Antony & Banuelas, 2002; Antony et al., 2007; Antony et al., 2008; Chakraborty & Tan, 2012; Jones et al., 2011; Kundi, 2005; Naslund, 2013; Tran, 2006; Wasage, 2012).

Upper management commitment to quality	5	Most Important	Similar	Same as above
Leadership and upper management support of Six Sigma budget	5	Most Important	Similar	Same as above
Using customers' concerns and feedback to improve quality	4	Very Important	Similar	(Antony, 2004; Antony & Banuelas, 2002; Antony et al., 2007; Kundi, 2005; Wasage, 2012).
Employee training on project management, statistical tools, quality commitment, teamwork, and DMAIC/DFSS	4	Very Important	Similar	Same as above

Open communication between management and employees of Six Sigma projects	4	Very Important	Similar	Same as above
Providing employee training to Six Sigma belts (Yellow Belt, Green Belt, Black Belt, Master Black Belt, Champion)	4	Very Important	Similar	Same as above
Offering rewards and recognition for Six Sigma project employees	3	Important	Similar	(Antony & Banuelas, 2002; Wasage, 2012).
Linking Six Sigma to suppliers (software vendors and material providers)	2	Less Important	Similar	Same as above

Six Sigma training during the hiring process	1	Least Important	Similar	Same as above
Training on Six Sigma to reduce employee turnover	1	Least Important	Similar	Same as above

As shown in Table 2, leadership commitment to Six Sigma, upper management commitment to quality, and leadership and upper management support of Six Sigma budget were identified as the most important CSFs. These findings were supported by previous similar Six Sigma research in business organizations (Achanga, 2006; Antony, 2004; Antony & Banuelas, 2002; Antony et al., 2007; Antony et al., 2008; Chakraborty & Tan, 2012; Jones, et al., 2011; Kundi, 2005; Naslund, 2013; Tran, 2005; Wasage, 2012).

Any successful initiative like Six Sigma requires leadership support (Antony & Banuelas, 2002). Leading U.S. companies that implemented and practiced Six Sigma noted that the most important CSF was persistent support and involvement from top leaders and upper management (Coronado & Antony, 2002). For example, Jack Welch, the former Chief Executive Officer of General Electric, strongly influenced and enabled the restructuring of the business organization and changed the attitude of the employees towards Six Sigma (Antony & Banuelas, 2002).

The levels of expectation in public work are low due to government bureaucracy (George, 2003). When former Mayor Richard began the Six Sigma quality initiative, none of the city staff had prior knowledge of quality improvement methodologies (George, 2003). However, Mayor Richard authorized numerous Six Sigma projects, encouraged employee training on Six Sigma and team building, required data collection, applied

DMAIC, and was actively involved in the city's implementation process (George, 2003). "It will take leadership consistency and persistence to convince people that life really has changed inside city government" (George, 2003, p. 140).

The analysis of Table 2 noted that using customers' concerns and feedback to improve quality, employee training on project management, statistical tools, quality commitment, teamwork, and DMAIC/DFSS, open communication between management and employees of Six Sigma projects, and providing employee training to Six Sigma belts (Yellow Belt, Green Belt, Black Belt, Master Black Belt, Champion) were very important CSFs. These findings were aligned with previous similar research in the private sector (Antony, 2004; Antony & Banuelas, 2002; Antony et al., 2007; Kundi, 2005; Wasage, 2012). It was not surprising that providing employee training to Six Sigma belts (Yellow Belt, Green Belt, Black Belt, Master Black Belt, and Champion) was a very important CSF. Under the Mayor's supervision, 30 employees were trained as

Black Belts and about 100 more were trained as Green Belts (Maleyeff, 2007).

It was not surprising that offering rewards and recognition for Six Sigma project employees was important. The results of the analysis also indicated that linking Six Sigma to suppliers (software vendors and material providers) was less important, followed by Six Sigma training during the hiring process, and training on Six Sigma to reduce employee turnover. These findings were also supported by previous similar studies in private organizations (Antony & Banuelas, 2002; Wasage, 2012).

These findings and the analysis of previous Six Sigma CSF research data (Achanga, 2006; Antony, 2004; Antony & Banuelas, 2002; Antony et al., 2007; Antony et al., 2008; Chakraborty & Tan, 2012; Jones et al., 2011; Kundi, 2005; Naslund, 2013; Tran, 2006; Wasage, 2012) revealed that leadership commitment to Six Sigma is the most important CSF. In addition, rank orders (relative importance) of CSFs on Six Sigma projects in both the private and public sectors display similar characteristics. Therefore, the following table indicates a summary of the hypothesis results:

| H1 | Leadership commitment to Six Sigma is the most important CSF in public sector Six Sigma-based projects. | Supported |
| H2 | Rank orders (relative importance) of CSFs on Six Sigma projects in both the private and public sectors display similar characteristics. | Supported |

As mentioned above, according to Coronado and Antony (2002), CSFs are those essential ingredients which are critical to the success of Six Sigma implementation. Without these CSFs, projects have little chance of success (Coronado and Antony, 2002). Six Sigma benefits, however, could be generated in three to five years (isixsigma.com, 2012; Pyzdek Institute, 2012). Therefore, managers should ensure that the implementation produces anticipated bottom line financial and non-financial benefits. Thus, it is also recommended that managers use Six Sigma metrics to evaluate anticipated implementation success (Coronado & Antony, 2002; isixsigma.com, 2012; Pyzdek Institute, 2012).

The most cited Six Sigma metrics include defect rate, financial measures (cost of quality, savings on rework and inspection costs, revenues, profits, and return on assets), customer satisfaction/customer complaints, quality of products/services, and production/service delivery time (Antony, 2004; Antony & Banuelas, 2002; Gillett et al., 2010; Ho & Chuang, 2006; Wasage, 2012). A survey conducted by Antony et al. (2007) indicated that Six Sigma in service organizations used the following metrics to evaluate anticipated implementation success: cost of poor quality (COPQ), defects per million opportunities (DPMO), time to respond to customer complaints, process capability, and number of customer complaints.

The respondent was asked about the effect of CSFs in the success of Six Sigma-based projects. It was interesting to note that Fort Wayne developed and used specific measurements of Outcome Based Budgeting (OBB) to complement Six Sigma metrics. OBB is a unique budgeting method that is devoted to identifying the targeted end results before allocating valuable financial and non-financial resources towards projects (Denhardt, 1999). From 2000 to 2008, Fort Wayne used OBB to analyze the effect of CSFs in the success of Six Sigma-based projects.

However, in Fort Wayne, public data showed that the city used some of the most cited performance metrics, such as cost savings and improved customer service. Since the introduction of Six Sigma, the city has saved $10-11 million, improved customer service, and increased productivity throughout the city (George, 2003; Leyh, 2009; Maleyeff, 2007). Another report also noted that the city saved $3 million in the first three years due to Six Sigma implementation (George, 2003). According to George (2003), the city used the following metrics to evaluate the effect of CSFs in the success of Six Sigma-based projects:

- By eliminating variation (an objective of Six Sigma) and bottlenecks, a Fire Department team performed 23 percent more reinspections each year without any increase in staffing. The length of time between reinspections, which was running in the hundreds of days at times, was reduced to an average of 34 days.
- Street pothole complaint response time was ranging up to 80 hours from notification to repair. As a result of Six Sigma implementation, 77 percent of the reported pothole repairs were made within 24 hours.
- A Park Department Black Belt project addressed citizen complaints. After improvement, the rate of complaint calls was reduced by 33 percent.

- About 35 percent of transportation engineering projects varied from their cost estimates by more than 10 percent, resulting in cash shortages. After improvement, only 14 percent of such projects exceed the cost estimates, resulting in increased cash flow of $150,000 over the first six months.

As indicated above, Six Sigma generated estimated savings of $10-11 million for the city (George, 2003; Leyh, 2009; Maleyeff, 2007). The initiative also improved customer satisfaction significantly (Maleyeff, 2007). From a political point view, Mayor Richard directed the Six Sigma program in the city since 2000 and he believed that his 16- percentage-point re-election win in 2004 was due to improved customer satisfaction (Maleyeff, 2007).

CONCLUSION

Budget shortfalls force local governments to do more with less. Fort Wayne, IN confronted these issues by improving efficiency in its processes (House, 2013). To do so, Fort Wayne leaders initiated and implemented Six Sigma. To successfully implement Six Sigma projects, organizations must use CSFs. CSFs are the essential components for the success of Six Sigma projects, because if these factors do not exist during the implementation, Six Sigma projects have little chance of generating net positive results (Antony et al., 2007; Kundi, 2005).

This paper presented a case study of the role of CSFs in Six Sigma implementation. These CSFs were analyzed using the city of Fort Wayne Six Sigma implementation process. The analysis revealed that leadership commitment to Six Sigma, upper management commitment to quality, and leadership and upper management support of Six Sigma budget were identified as the "most important" CSFs. These findings were supported by previous studies (Achanga, 2006; Antony, 2004; Antony & Banuelas, 2002; Antony et al., 2007; Antony et al., 2008; Chakraborty & Tan, 2012; Jones et al., 2011; Kundi, 2005; Naslund, 2013; Tran, 2005; Wasage, 2012).

Former Mayor Richard directed the Six Sigma effort and devoted considerable energy to the Six Sigma efforts (Maleyeff, 2007). The analysis also found that providing employee training to Six Sigma belts (Yellow Belt, Green Belt, Black Belt, Master Black Belt, and Champion) was another "very important" CSF. As noted before, under the

Mayor's supervision, 30 employees were trained as Black Belts and about 100 more were trained as Green Belts (Maleyeff, 2007).

The analysis also found that Six Sigma training during the hiring process and training on Six Sigma to reduce employee turnover were the "least important" CSFs. In addition, the analysis suggested that rank orders (relative importance) of CSFs on Six Sigma projects in both the private and public sectors displayed similar characteristics. These findings were aligned with previous Six Sigma studies in business organizations (Achanga, 2006; Antony, 2004; Antony & Banuelas, 2002; Antony et al., 2007; Antony et al., 2008; Chakraborty & Tan, 2012; Jones et al., 2011; Kundi, 2005; Naslund, 2013; Tran, 2005; Wasage, 2012). In addition, analysis found that the city used OBB to evaluate the effect of CSFs on the success of Six Sigma based projects. Public data, however, indicated that the city used some of the most frequently cited performance metrics, such as project savings, customer complaints/satisfaction, and production/service delivery time to evaluate the effect of CSFs on the success of Six Sigma based projects.

Based on the study, the following recommendations were proposed:

- Leadership commitment to Six Sigma is the "most important" CSF. Leadership can mitigate employee resistance and encourage training. Also, leadership can cut unnecessary bureaucratic structures (in Fort Wayne, a permit approval process had 14 different agencies) to improve delivery time. Thus, top management must be on aboard first. However, successful Six Sigma implementation depends upon all of the CSFs. Therefore, once top management is on aboard, the other CSFs should be presented. If any of the CSFs is missing, the company may be wasting money, time, and resources because in order to achieve the full potential of Six Sigma, it is vital to take all CSFs into consideration (Coronado & Antony, 2002).

- Elected officials should understand that performance is the best politics for reelection (Denhardt, 1999). Thus, they should realize that Six Sigma can produce savings, improve service/product delivery time, and enhance processes.
- Public sector organizations usually do not have any prior quality improvement culture.

Therefore, Six Sigma training helps employees to improve their comfort level through classes and training, and it also helps motivate employees to overcome resistance (Antony & Banuelas, 2002). Thus, an organization should use the certified belt hierarchy (Yellow Belt, Green Belt, Black Belt, Master Black Belt, and Champion) system as a criterion to evaluate employees' reviews and promotions.

- Consistent internal communication between management and employees is very important for the success of Six Sigma implementation (Coronado & Antony, 2002; Wasage, 2012).
- Most government employees go into government for public service and they like

to be recognized for their contributions to the public service (Denhardt, 1999). Public sector organizations often do not offer financial bonuses and incentives (Denhardt, 1999). Therefore, non-financial rewards, incentives, and recognitions are important factors to motivate employees.

- Six Sigma implementation costs may exceed expected benefits in the beginning. Six Sigma, however, is not a get rich quick magic bullet (Pyzdek Institute, 2012). Six Sigma is a journey, not a destination (Pande et al., 2000; Pyzdek Institute, 2012). It will take at least three to five years to see Six Sigma benefits such cost savings, improving customer satisfaction, and improving processes.

LIMITATIONS OF THE STUDY

Several limitations to the current study were identified. Notably, Six Sigma is still a new concept to local governments. As a result, there are only a few local governments that have implemented Six Sigma. This case study holistically investigated (all Six Sigma projects together) the impact of CSFs on the implementation process in Fort Wayne. In order to have a deeper understanding of a specific Six Sigma project (for example, one particular department project), future researchers can select a particular Six Sigma project (Antony, 2004; Antony & Banuelas, 2002; Antony et al., 2007; Antony et al., 2008; Wasage, 2012).

In order to achieve research objectives, five quality professionals were contacted. Although follow-up phone calls were conducted, only one interview was granted and completed. To avoid low response rates, future research can conduct several semi-structured interviews and surveys to enhance reliability (Antony, 2004; Antony & Banuelas, 2002; Antony et al., 2007; Antony et al., 2008; Wasage, 2012). While the respondent was in a good position (participated in 60 projects) to identify rank orders of CSFs and their impact, the respondent's perspective on Six Sigma implementation was not without bias.

The results presented in the study were from a single organization (City of Fort Wayne, IN). Future research is needed to generalize these findings. Despite some limitations, the study theoretically and practically contributes to the Six Sigma literature because prior to this study, scholars have shown little interest in conducting a study on the influence of CSFs on Six Sigma implementation in local governments. This research has narrowed this gap in the Six Sigma literature.

References

Achanga, P. (2006). Critical success factors for lean implementation with SMEs. *Journal of Manufacturing Technology Management, 17*(4), 460-471.

Anbari, F. T., & Kwak, Y. H. (2004, July). *Success factors in managing Six Sigma projects.* Paper presented at the Project Management Research Conference, London, UK.

Antony, J. (2004). Six Sigma in the UK service organizations: Result from a pilot survey. *Managerial Auditing Journal, 19*(8), 1006-1013.

Antony, J., Antony, F. J., Kumar, M., & Cho, B. R., (2007). Six Sigma in service organizations: Benefits, challenges and difficulties, common myths, empirical observations and success factors. *International Journal of the Quality and Reliability Management, 24*(3), 294-311.

Antony, J., & Banuelas, R. (2002). Key ingredients for the effective implementation of Six Sigma program. Measuring Business Excellence, 6(4), 20-27.

Antony, J., Kumar, M., & Labib, A. (2008). Gearing Six Sigma into UK manufacturing SMEs: Results from a pilot study. *Journal of the Operation Research Society, 59*(4), 482-493.

Babbie, E. (1986). The practice of social research. Belmont, CA: Wadsworth Publishing Company.

Benest, F. (n.d.). *Serving customers or engaging citizens*. Retrieved from http://newcity.ca/Pages/benest.html

Bowman, A.O. M., & Kearney, R. C. (2010). *State and local government*. Boston, MA: Wadsworth Cengage Learning.

Boyne, G., & Walker, R. (2002). Total quality management and performance, an evaluation of the evidence and lessons for research on public organizations. *Public Performance & Management Review 26*(2), 111-131.

Buthmann, A. (2010, September 2). *Cost of quality: Not only failure costs*. Retrieved from http://isixsigma.com

Center for Association Leadership. (2011). *Is Social Responsibility Our Responsibility?* Retrieved from http://www.asaecenter.org/Resources/JALArticleDetail.cfm?ItemNumber=19975&pg=5

Chakraborty, A. & Tan, K. C. (2012). Case study analysis of Six Sigma implementation in service organizations. *Business Process Management Journal, 18*(6), 992-1018.

City of Coral Springs. (2014). Our quality initiative. Retrieved from http://www.coralsprings.org/quality/

City of Fort Wayne. (2007). Mayor to be keynote speaker at national Six Sigma conference. Retrieved from https://www.cityoffortwayne.org/latest-news/1070-mayor-to-be-keynote-speaker-at-national-six-sigma-conference.html

Coronado, R. B., & Antony, J. (2002). Critical success factors for the successful implementation of Six Sigma projects in organizations. *The TQM Magazine, 14*(2), 92-99.

Deming, W. E. (1986). *Out of the crisis.* Cambridge, MA: Massachusetts Institute of Technology, Center for Advanced Engineering Study.

Denhardt, R. B. (1999). *Public administration: An action orientation.* Orlando, FL: Harcourt Brace.

Eckes, G. (2000). *The Six Sigma Revolution: How General Electric and others turned process into profits.* New York, NY: John Wiley & Sons.

Edwards, D. (2011). *Smarter, faster, cheaper: An operations efficiency benchmarking study of 100 American cities.* Retrieved from

http://public.dhe.ibm.com/common/ssi/ecm/
en/gbw03132usen/GBW03132USEN.PDF

Furterer, S., & Elshennawy, A., K. (2005). Implementation of TQM and lean Six Sigma tools in local government: A framework and a case study. *Total Quality Management & Business Excellence, 16*(10), 1179-1191.

George, M., L. (2003). Lean Six Sigma for service: How to use lean speed and Six Sigma quality to improve services and transactions. New York City, NY: McGraw Hill.

Gillett, J., Fink, R., & Bevington, N. (2010, April). How Caterpillar uses 6 Sigma to execute strategy. *Strategic Finance,* 25-28.

Greene, C. M., Ellis, B., Waller, M., & Osborne, M. (2008). *Six Sigma in the 21 century.* Paper presented at the Industrial Engineering Research Conference, Vancouver, Canada.

Gupta, N. (2013). An overview on Six Sigma: Quality improvement program. *International Journal of Technical Research and Applications, 1*(1), 29-39.

Harry, M., & Schroeder, R. (2000). *Six Sigma: The breakthrough strategy revolutionizing the world's top corporations.* New York, NY: Doubleday.

Hartley, J. (2004). Case study research. In C. Cassell & G. Symon (Eds.), *Essential guide to qualitative methods in organizational research* (pp. 323-333). London: Sage Publications.

Hekmatpanah, M., Sadroddin, M., Shahbaz, S., Mokhtari, F., & Fadavinia, F. (2008), Six

Sigma process and its impact on the organization productivity. *International Journal of Social, Behavioral, Educational, Economic, Business and Industrial Engineering, 7*, 731-735.

Hellein, R., & Bowman, J. (2002). The process of quality management implementation: State government agencies in Florida. *Public Performance & Management Review Journal, 26*(1), 75-93.

Ho, L. H., & Chuang, C. C. (2006). A study of implementing Six Sigma quality management system in government agencies for raising service quality. *The Journal of American Academy of Business, 10*(1), 167-173.

House, J. (2013, October 23). U.S. cities still reeling from great recession. *The Wall Street Journal*. Retrieved from http://blogs.wsj.com/economics/2013/10/23/u-s-cities-still-reeling-from-great-recession/

isixsigma. (2012). *New to learn Six Sigma*. Retrieved from http://www.isixsigma.com/index.php?option=com_content&view=article&id=201&Iemid=27

Jones, E. C., Parast, M. M., & Adams, S. G. (2011). Developing an instrument for measuring Six Sigma implementation. *International Journal of Services and Operations Management, 9*(4), 429-452.

Jones, R., G. (1999). *Organizational theory.* Reading, MA: Addison-Wesley.

Kundi, O. H. K., (2005). *A study of Six Sigma implementation and critical success factors.* Paper presented at Pakistan's 9th International Convention on Quality Improvement Conference, Lahore, Pakistan.

Lambert, L. (2013, February 28). *U.S. cities face threats from federal cuts to revenues, economies.* Retrieved from http://www.reuters.com/article/2013/02/28/usa-fiscal-cities idUSL1N0BSLW820130228

Leyh, T (2009). *Efficient government through Lean Six Sigma.* Retrieved from http://icma.org/Documents/QuestionAnswer/Document/7554

Luengo, O. D. (2004). *Six Sigma in Action: A Case Study Analysis* (Doctoral dissertation). Retrieved from ProQuest Dissertations and Theses.

Maleyeff, J. (2007). *Improving service delivery in government with Lean Six Sigma*. Retrieved from http://www.doh.wa.gov/Portals/1/Documents/1000/PMC-ImproveServiceDeliveryLeanSixSigmaReport.pdf

Moosa, K., & Sajid, A. (2010). Critical analysis of Six Sigma implementation. *Total Quality Management, 21*(7), 745-759.

Mukkamala, H. K. (2013). *Critical Success Factors for the Implementation of PeopleSoft Enterprise Resource Planning in a Public*

Organization (Doctoral dissertation). Retrieved from ProQuest Dissertations and Theses.

Nachmias, F. C., & Nachimias, D. (1996). *Research methods in the social sciences.* New York, NY: St. Martin's Press.

Naslund, D. (2013). Lean and Six Sigma-Critical success factors revisited. *International Journal of Quality and Service Science, 5*(1), 86-100.

Pande, P. S., Neuman, R. P., & Cavanagh, R. R. (2000). *The Six Sigma way: How GE, Motorola, and other top companies are honing their performance.* New York, NY: McGraw-Hill.

Pavletic, D., & Sokovic, M. (2002). The Lean and Six Sigma synergy. *International Journal for Quality Research, 2*(4), 247-256.

Pyzdek, T. (2014). Despite success, lean Six Sigma ending in Erie County. Retrieved from https://www.sixsigmatraining.org/news-blog/despite-success-lean-six-sigma-ending-in-erie-county.html

Pyzdek Institute (2012). Six Sigma questions and answers. Retrieved from http://www.sixsigmatraining.org/sixsigmafaqs

Richard, G. (2005). *Letter from the mayor.* City of Fort Wayne. Retrieved from http://www.cityoffortwayne.org/component/content/article/72-controllers-office/527-letter-from-the-mayor-.html

Robinson, V (2001). *Best practice: Fort Wayne adopts Six Sigma methodology to improve city services.* The United States Conference of Mayors. Retrieved from http://www.usmayors.org/usmayornewspaper/documents/06_11_01/ft_wayne_best_practice.asp

Sawicky, B. S. (2002). U.S. cities face fiscal crunch: Federal and state policies exacerbate local governments' budget shortfalls. *Economic Policy Institute*, 181. Retrieved from http://www.epi.org/publication/issuebriefs_ib181/

Shah, R. R., Chandrasekaran, A. A., & Linderman, K. K. (2008). In pursuit of implementation patterns: The context of Lean and Six

Sigma. *International Journal of Production Research*, *46*(23), 6679-6699

Tjahjono, B., Ball, P., Vitanov, V. I., Scorzafave, C., Nogueira, J., Calleja, M., Minguet, L., Narasimha, L., Riva, A., Srivastava, A., Srivastava, S., Yadav, A. (2010). Six Sigma: A literature review: *International Journal of Lean Six Sigma*, *1*(3), 216-232.

Tran, D. (2006). *Factors in the successful implementation of Six Sigma in Canadian manufacturing firms.* (Master Thesis). Retrieved from ProQuest Dissertations and Theses. (UMI No. 305353567).

Turban, E., Sharda., R., Aronson, J. E., & King, D. (2008). *Business intelligence: A managerial approach*. Upper Saddle River, NJ: Prentice Hall.

Valenzuela, D. & Shrivastava, P. (n.d). Interview as a Method for Qualitative Research [PowerPoint slides]. Retrieved from http://www.public.asu.edu/~kroel/www500/Interview%20Fri.pdf

Wasage, C. (2012). *Measuring the effectiveness of Six Sigma implementation in Fortune 500 companies: An Empirical Study* (Doctoral dissertation). Retrieved from ProQuest Dissertations and Theses. (AAT 3549811)

Watson, G.H., & deYong, C.F. (2010). Design for Six Sigma: Caveat emptor. *International Journal of Lean Six Sigma, 1*(1), 66-84.

Yin, R. K. (2003). *Case Study Research: Design and Methods*. London: Sage Publications Inc.

Author Biography

Chamith Wasage is an adjunct professor of Business Management at Bellevue University, Bellevue, NE. He received his Doctorate in Business Administration (DBA) from Wilmington University, Wilmington, DE. He also holds a bachelor's degree (BS) in Accounting from Bellevue University, Bellevue, NE; master's degree (MBA) in Business Administration from Bellevue University, Bellevue, NE; master's degree (MS) in Urban Studies from the University of Nebraska at Omaha, NE; master's degree (MPA) in Public Administration from the University of Nebraska at Omaha, NE.

Dr. Wasage's recent research appeared in *Journal of Modern Accounting and Auditing* (Implementation of Six Sigma Projects in Fortune 500 Companies). Dr. Wasage's dissertation was also focused on Six Sigma projects (Measuring the effectiveness of six sigma implementation in fortune 500 companies: An empirical study).

www.ingramcontent.com/pod-product-compliance
Lightning Source LLC
Chambersburg PA
CBHW020450220526
45464CB00002B/939